REPRINTS OF ECONOMIC CLASSICS

IMPOLICY OF A BOUNTY ON THE
EXPORTATION OF GRAIN

Also published in

Reprints of Economic Classics

by James Mill

Commerce Defended [1808]
Elements of Political Economy [1844]

AN

ESSAY

OF THE

IMPOLICY OF A BOUNTY

ON THE

EXPORTATION OF GRAIN

[JAMES MILL]

[1804]

REPRINTS OF ECONOMIC CLASSICS

AUGUSTUS M. KELLEY · PUBLISHERS
NEW YORK · 1966

LIBRARY OF CONGRESS CATALOGUE CARD NUMBER
66 - 19693

PRINTED IN THE UNITED STATES OF AMERICA
by SENTRY PRESS, NEW YORK, N. Y. 10019

AN
ESSAY

OF THE

IMPOLICY OF A BOUNTY

ON THE

EXPORTATION OF GRAIN;

AND

ON THE PRINCIPLES

WHICH OUGHT TO REGULATE THE

COMMERCE OF GRAIN,

DIVIDED UNDER THE FOLLOWING HEADS:

Of the History of the Corn Laws; Influence of the Population on the Corn-Trade; Effects of the Bounty on the Rent of Lands; Effects of the Bounty on the Profits of the Farmer; Effects of the Bounty on the Value of Silver; Exportation; Importation; Landlords, Farmers, and Corn Dealers.

LONDON:

PRINTED FOR C. & R. BALDWIN, NEW-BRIDGE-STREET;
Sold also by W. Ginger of Piccadilly; W. J. & J. Richardson,
and J. Asperne of Cornhill; and by P. Hill, and
J. Anderson, Edinburgh.

1804.
(Price 2s/10d.) *p mail coach*

ADVERTISEMENT.

A CONSIDERABLE part of this Essay was presented to the Public a short time since in the LITERARY JOURNAL, in the Review of a Pamphlet by Dr. Anderson. It afterwards appeared to the Author that the reasonings contained in that article might be further illustrated and extended; and that, if they were just, it was of some importance at the present moment that they should be made as generally known as possible. These considerations have produced the present performance.

INTRODUCTION.

CORN, being the only necessary article, is affected by certain circumstances which render the trade in Corn somewhat more complicated and mysterious than the ordinary cases of trade. This obscurity however might be easily removed, if the real difficulties of the subject were all that we had to contend with. But a number of theories have been formed with regard to it; these have taken possession of people's minds, and to remove these is the first, and probably the greatest task which we have to perform, to diffuse a general knowledge of the principles which ought to regulate this important branch of the national affairs.

The great object is to procure a proper supply of the necessaries of life. During the scarcity which we endured in this country a few years ago, the minds of men were more turned to the subject than they had been before. By the inquiries then made it appeared that during the last forty years this country had not raised all the Corn necessary for its own subsistence; and it was known that during all periods the country had been occasionally subject to the disadvantages and miseries of scarcity. There were two evils therefore existing in this department of the national interests; that of being, in some measure, dependent upon

our neighbours for the necessaries of life; and
that of being liable to the hardships of scarcity.
It was the policy of the State to contrive means
for removing both of those disadvantages. They
were acknowledged to be disadvantages of the
greatest magnitude.

It was properly, and naturally, the chief object
of concern, during the pressure of that scarcity,
to find the means of redressing the evils immediately felt. The first of these was the importation of the article wanted. But various other
measures were talked of. One became so much
applauded that Mr. Burke, a very short time before his death, thought it necessary, in a memo-
rial presented to Mr. Pitt, to prove the utter impolicy of it, under immediate fear that it was
about to be adopted by the legislature. This was
to fix by authority the rate of labourers' wages,
according to the price of corn; it being understood that at the rate of wages, and the price of
corn then existing, the labourer was unable to
procure the means of subsistence, and that the
farmer was making extraordinary and unreasonable
gains.

Besides the means of removing the evils immediately felt, the means were sought of preventing
the recurrence of scarcity. For this object also
one contrivance, that of public granaries, became
so much a favourite, that Mr. Burke thought it
necessary to warn the public against it in that
performance to which I have already alluded, and

in which he has told us many things, which it is to be lamented so few of us seem to know.

While such projects were devised for removing scarcity, the second of the evils above-mentioned, and for preventing its recurrence, our attention was attracted, in some degree, to the first of those objects too, our dependance upon foreign countries for a part of our supply; and various schemes for the improvement of agriculture were daily discussed. The return of plenty put an end to those speculations; and we should have gone on without any further inquiry, till a new scarcity had overtaken us, if it had not been for an effect of the preceding scarcity which began to be experienced.

During the reign of enormous prices and of high profits, it is well known that the ideas of the farmers became too high. They estimated, as was not unnatural, at much more than its proper value, the continuance of the gains they were then making. They were so eager in their business that they became willing to promise any rent for their farms. New leases were in almost all cases granted upon terms proportioned, or nearly proportioned to the price of corn at that time. When the price of corn fell they found themselves of necessity reduced to distress, having bound themselves in an unwise, and unequal contract. But, as is usual with men, they did not blame themselves for the evils which they felt; they blamed the low price to which corn had fallen; and one of the happiest circumstances which could arrive to this country became the object of their clamour and outcry. The farmers had not sufficient profits; they could not carry on their trade; prices must be raised. Of course the landlords liked this cry much better, than that against unreasonable and ruinous leases. They joined in it; for their interest naturally prevented them from seeing its absurdity. They came to parliament for assistance to export corn, till the farmers could sell it high enough to pay them their present rents; and, wonderful to tell, parliament granted that assistance!

Of course it was not for the declared purpose of enabling them to draw great rents that they sought or obtained the law. The old mercantile theory of politics suggested certain vague ideas of the efficacy of bounties; and they persuaded parliament, and endeavoured to persuade the world, that to grant a bounty on the exportation of corn, and a duty on importation, was one of the most effectual means to promote the interests of the country.

The advocates for the law enacted upon these reasons tell us, that the effects of a bounty upon the exportation of corn are to encourage in such a manner the production of corn, that in all ordinary years we shall not only supply ourselves, but have a surplus to export, and that in deficient years we shall have this surplus in reserve, to prevent the effects of scarcity; that the happy con-

sequence of this law therefore will be a deliverance
from both the evils under which we labour, of
being dependent upon our neighbours for the necessaries of life, and of being subject to the hardships and dangers of scarcity. '

This is unquestionably a very lofty promise.
It is not a trifling benefit which the inventors of
this expedient will have the honour of bestowing
upon their country. Their merit is not diminished
by the simplicity of the means employed to attain
so important an end. But it may be reckoned
somewhat wonderful, that a discovery of this
magnitude should so long have escaped the intel-
lectual eyes of all the great men who have spent
their days in studying the means of national prosperity; and should be reserved to distinguish and
immortalize those profound thinkers, and indefa-
tigable inquirers who brought forward the late
corn law. From the infinite diligence with which
they have been long known to study all the pro-
foundest questions of political economy, it was to
be expected that they would go much deeper
than any of their predecessors; and things of no
small importance which had escaped all who
went before them we justly hoped that they
would bring to light. But a discovery so extraordinary as this even the great hopes which they
had raised did not entitle us to expect. So much
the greater therefore are our obligations.

They present their reasons to us in abundance
of words, and they are composed of various par-

ticulars. They may all however be reduced to
two heads; and it will assist us in obtaining a
clear idea of them to consider them under that
division. The first may be denominated their
argument from *experience*; the second their argument from the nature of the case. Under these
heads will be included every thing which has been
advanced in favour of the bounty upon exportation by Dirom and Mackie, by Dr. Anderson, and
Mr. Malthus, and indeed every thing which the
author of this essay conceives it to be possible to
adduce in behalf of this doctrine. It s his intention to examine these arguments in every light
in which they can be presented. And he has dis-
tributed the different parts of that examination
under separate titles in the chapters which follow.

ESSAY

ON

THE CORN LAWS.

CHAP. I.

Of the History of the Corn Laws.

To prove from *experience* the good effects of granting a bounty on the exportation of corn and of imposing a duty on importation, the advocates for that measure give us a chronological account of the corn trade, from the time of Edward the 3d. It will contribute to distinctness, if I make a division of this period. In the year 1688, a law was passed for the first time, granting a bounty on the exportation of corn, and imposing a duty on importation. This law continued in force till about the year 1770, when it was in a great measure repealed. And since the year 1770, the exportation of corn has scarcely been encouraged. We may therefore consider the history of the corn trade, as comprehending three great periods; 1st. That preceding the enactment of the exportation law in 1688; 2d. The period during which that law was in force; and 3d. The period during which that law has been repealed. According to this division we may state the argument from experience, adduced by the patrons of the law, very shortly, thus:

During the first period, exportation was either not permitted at all, or was at least burthened with a duty. No register was kept of exports and imports during this period; so that no conclusion can be drawn from the balance of this account, with regard to the quantity of corn produced. But we have a register of prices. During the last forty years of this period, the average price of the quarter of wheat was £2 14s. 9d. whereas during forty years posterior to 1720, while the law of 1688 was in full force, the price of the quarter of wheat was £1 16s. 2d. This is sufficient to prove that the cultivation of corn was much more prosperous during the latter than during the former period.

At the commencement of the second period, a bounty for the first time was granted upon the exportation of corn; and importation was subjected to a duty, or altogether prohibited. During this period our exports of corn rose greatly above our imports; and at the same time the price of corn was very low.

During the last period, the operation of this law of bounty on exportation and duty on importation has not been steady; sometimes it has been suspended, sometimes permitted, and sometimes even inverted. And during this period our exportation of corn has fallen greatly below our importation, and the price of corn has become very high.

It appears then, that during the time when the law of bounty was in full·force, the exportation of corn was great, and the price low; and that during the times both before and after, when that law was not in full force, the exportation was little or none, and the price high. From this they conclude that to grant a bounty on the exportation of corn, and to impose a duty on the importation, is proved by experience to be wise and politic.

No arguments are more satisfactory than those from experience when the conclusions are legitimate. But no species of false reasoning is more deceitful than that from experience; nor is any more common. Lord Bacon, the great father of the Philosophy of Experience well understood this source of error; and when he divided all false philosophy into three species, he represented those who reason fallaciously from experience as composing, the second of the three classes; and their errors, he said, were still more monstrous and deformed than those of the hypothetical, or speculative philosophers. Some of the greatest and most fatal errors which have ever been offered to the world have been the fruit of an imperfect argument from experience. Such was Mr. Hume's famous argument against Christianity. This too was the origin of the monstrous doctrines of Mr. Hobbes both in religion and politics. How often does false reasoning from the immoral lives of persons who profess to be very religious lead others to become infidels? or how often does false reasoning, from the abuses observed in the management of existing governments, lead people to wish for the subversion of government? What was it but an argument from experience of this sort which brought forward all the horrors of the French revolution? Nothing is more common, since the honours of the experimental philosophy were so generally acknowledged, than to find shallow thinkers bring forward their arguments from experience on every subject. Among the common herd too of readers or hearers you very often find them with the most absurd pretensions of this sort gaining absolute credit. There is no species of pretension, however, against which the man of sense ought to be more on his guard. He will find, if he takes the trouble to examine, that one half of the popular errors which at present prevail are derived from no other source.

When we come to examine a little closely this experience of the advocates for the exportation bounty, we find it to consist in the single circumstance of being co-temporary. The low price of corn, and a great exportation was co-temporary with the law for the bounty; and this is all. To make their argument good then, they must prove that every thing which is co-temporary with another, is absolutely owing to that other. The national debt began about the very time when the bounty law was passed. Do they maintain therefore that the exportation and low price of corn during 50 years was owing to the existence and progress of the national debt? A very pretty theory however we think might be formed on this idea. It is the opinion of a numerous class of speculators, that a national debt is advantageous; but that it may be increased so far as to become burthensome and ruinous. Now observe; Great Britain had a national debt from the beginning of the eighteenth century; it went on gradually till the middle of that century, and during that time she continued to export corn and the price of it fell; but about that time the national debt passed the bounds of propriety, and ever since, the importation of corn has increased, and the price has risen. Is not this a demonstration from experience, that a national debt is advantageous till it amount to a certain sum, and is disadvantageous when it goes beyond that sum? It was not from any idea of assistance to the cultivation of corn, or any intention to benefit the nation, that the king's ministers in 1688 proposed, and obtained the law for granting a bounty on the exportation of corn. We are expressly informed in the history of that time, that it was passed to give a premium to the country gentlemen, in order to obtain their consent to the imposition of the land tax. This land tax, therefore, has been co-temporary with the bounty law. Accordingly we may argue that the prosperous state of the corn trade, during the period described, was owing to the land tax. The only very disastrous period too of that trade has been since the alteration was introduced into the state of the land tax. The benefit of the land tax then for the encouragement of agriculture is fully proved. I see not why the poor laws should not be entitled to the same distinction. They were in full force during all the time of this prosperity. Some time ago, however, Mr. Pitt introduced certain alterations of the poor laws ; and since agriculture has been terribly on the decline. Agriculture has never flourished too since the sinking fund was established ; indeed it has declined ever since his present Majesty came to the throne. But it flourished greatly during the reigns of the first two princes of the Brunswick line. Why, therefore, should we not conclude that the existence of those two princes was very favourable to agriculture, but that the existence of the last is very unfavourable to it? Or what if we should say, that the administration of Sir Robert Walpole, the Duke of Newcastle, &c. was very favourable to agriculture, but that of Mr. Pitt is very unfavourable to it; let us, therefore, have done with him, that we may export plenty of corn, and have it cheap! Were nothing more proposed than to refute the patrons of the bounty law, what has been already said, is fully sufficient to shew the futility of their argument from experience. But as it is of importance that the public should receive as complete information as possible, respecting a subject so interesting as this, I shall examine a little more particularly the different periods which I have assigned ; and we shall see whether the circumstances of the times do not point out to us causes of the variations in the state of the corn trade, altogether different from the law of exportation.

In the first period, the 40 years immediately preceding the year 1688, are particularly specified. This was that period of tumult, contention, distraction, and distress which succeeded the death of Charles the First ; the period of the Protectorate, during which the affairs of the nation were in a state of so much derangement ; and that of the reigns of Charles the Second and James the Second, during which the nation was kept in continual agitation by the fears of popery and arbitrary power. The unhappy circumstances of those times are surely sufficient and more than sufficient to account for the state of the corn trade, which was not more unprosperous than any other branch of national affairs. We have therefore no reason whatever to have recourse to the want of a bounty on the exportation of corn, to explain all the appearances in this first period.

The second period began with the establishment of that admirable constitution, of that balanced system of liberty and coercion, which unites the freedom and the protection of the individual more effectually than has ever yet been done by

any other government on the face of the earth.
This extraordinary advantage gave an encouragement to every species of industry which could not
fail to be speedily and powerfully felt. It was felt
accordingly; and the nation went forward in a
career of prosperity, of which there is hardly any
example. Agriculture experienced the first effects
of the happy change, as necessarily happened
from the circumstances in which the country was
placed. Agriculture was that species of industry
which was then best known in the nation, and to
which the greatest capital was applied. Manufactures, at least for foreign trade, had previous to
this time been very little known. During the
tempestuous period too which preceded, when the
security of property was greatly impaired, the capital employed in manufactures was the most easily
dispersed ; and manufacturing industry and enter-
prize, being most easily discouraged and checked,
necessarily suffered more in proportion than the
more hardy and indispensable business of agriculture. Agriculture then was in a much better condition to take advantage of the happy circumstances of the revolution; and advanced with very
rapid strides for many years. Whoever considers
duly these circumstances will not be surprized at
the prosperous state of agriculture during this
period. He will not find any occasion to account
for it by any extraordinary cause, as that of a
bounty on exportation. He will rather, if he is
surprised at any thing in the case, wonder that,

great as the prosperity was, it was not still greater. It will not then I think be denied that all the appearances of the first two periods which afford our experience of the corn trade, may be completely accounted for without the operation of the bounty law.

But what, it may be asked, can be said with regard to the third period ? The operation of that law was interrupted during this period, and the prosperity of the Corn trade declined. To what other cause could this be owing but to the want of the duty on exportation? Let me finish the historical sketch which I have begun, and a cause will appear which will probably be judged satisfactory. While agriculture was advancing in the manner I have above described, all other branches of national industry began, from the same causes, to make progress. The movements of commerce were feeble at the beginning, from the extreme state of debility in which they began. It gathered strength however every day ; and in a short time its progress appeared evidently to be more rapid than that of agriculture. Agriculture was greatly before commerce at the beginning of the century; but commerce continued to gain ground till toward the middle of the century, or perhaps a little after the middle ; when it may be fairly reckoned to have got the start, and it has continued to increase its distance ever since. Whoev eris acquainted with the 3d book of the Nature and Causes of the Wealth of Nations, in which

Dr. Smith explains so admirably how much more
commerce has been encouraged in modern Europe
than agriculture, will be at no loss to account for
the more rapid progress of commerce than that
of agriculture in Great Britain during the last century.

Of the different states of thing here described
the necessary effects were these ; during the time
that agriculture kept before commerce, the produce
of argriculture was more than sufficient to supply
all those who were employed in agriculture, and
those who were employed in manufactures, and in
the other business of the nation ; it furnished
therefore a surplus to export ; but when commerce
on the other hand advanced greatly before agriculture, then agriculture could no longer afford
enough to maintain all those who were employed
in manufactures and the other business of the
nation, and a deficiency remained to be supplied
by importation. This is the cause that since the
middle of the last century our importation of corn
has exceeded our exportation, and not the temporary suspensions of the bounty on exportation.

If this conclusion be just, all the appearances in
the three periods into which they divide the history
of the corn trade are then fully accounted for; and
the bounty on exportation had nothing to do with
them. Let us examine still farther if there is any
objection which they can possibly bring to that
conclusion. They cannot pretend to doubt that
this country was much farther back as a manufac-

turing country than as an agricultural country at
the time of the revolution. This is a point which
is too well known to admit of any dispute. They
will readily admit too that this country is now
much farther forward as a manufacturing country
than as an agricultural country; for this is the
thing of which they complain. The particular
point of time likewise at which manufacturing industry got before agricultural, they will probably
be willing to grant, was that time when exportation
of corn began to be changed for importation. We
are agreed then with regard to all the facts. We
can only dispute therefore concerning causes.
Perhaps they will say that the manufacturing business got the start of the agricultural, not on
account of those general discouragements imposed
upon agriculture, which are so ably illustrated by
Dr. Smith, and to which we have referred; but on
account of the suspension of the bounty on the
exportation of corn. If we saw two ships, the
one a great way behind the other, but sailing in
the same direction; if we saw too that the last was
the fastest sailer, and gradually advanced upon the
other, till at last she overtook her; and if we saw that
at this time the slow sailing vessel dropt a sail, and
the fast sailing vessel advanced before her, but did
not increase her distance any faster than she diminished it before, should we say that the lowering
of that sail was in any degree the cause why the
fast sailing vessel got before the slow sailing one?
Surely not. As the comparative velocity of the

two ships was exactly the same both before and after that sail was down, we cannot assign to it any influence whatever in the progress of either.

During the first part of the last century, the bounty on the exportation of corn was in full force ; during the latter part it was interrupted. But if it appears that the progress of manufacturing industry in its advancement upon agricultural was just as rapid during the time the bounty was operating, as it was in getting before agricultural industry after the bounty was interrupted, it will be ridiculous to ascribe the more rapid motion of manufacturing industry to the want of the bounty on the exportation of corn. Because it will appear that this motion is equally rapid both when the bounty acts, and when it does not act. We have fortunately a series of facts which place this matter beyond all doubt, and prove most decisively that it is not to the bounty on the exportation of corn that we are to ascribe the comparatively slow progress of agricultural industry.

Let us observe the comparative progress of agricultural and commercial industry, during the period when the bounty on the exportation of corn was operating. The test to which the example of the advocates for the bounty leads us to apply is the account of the exports and imports. In the year 1697, the first in which a register was kept of the quantity of corn exported and imported, the excess of the exports above the imports was 101,643 quarters : in the same year the general exports from Great Britain, including this corn, were £3,525,906

official value. In the year 1764, the last year of
the full operation of the corn bounty, the excess of
the exports above the imports of corn was 535,528
quarters ; and in the same year the general exports
from Great Britain amounted to £17,756,331 ;
that is to say, during this period of nearly 70 years,
the corn trade exhibits an improvement of about
400,000 quarters for one year, worth not so much
as £800,000, while the general commerce of the
country exhibits an improvement of more than
fourteen millions. Such then was the comparative
progress of commercial and agricultural industry,
while the bounty on the exportation of corn was in
full operation ; the progress of commercial industry was many times more rapid than that of agricultural. Let us next observe what was the case
after the operation of the bounty was interrupted.
I shall only examine it down to the commencement
of the war with republican France, because the extraordinary changes then experienced are not to be
explained according to the ordinary course of
events. The general exports from Great Britain
then in the year 1792 amounted to £24,905,200.
This compared with the account of the exports in
1764, exhibits an improvement of rather more
than seven millions in thirty years, which is almost exactly the rate of improvement during the
period in which the bounty operated. I have not immediately before me the state of the corn trade for
the precise year 1792, but I have an account of the
average of the five years immediately preceding.

That makes the excess of imports amount to 411,819 quarters. This added to the 535,528 quarters exported in 1764, makes a difference of 947,347 quarters. But let us recollect what has to be done with this quantity of corn. It has to maintain all the persons who are employed in preparing merchandise for exportation to the amount of seven millions annually; for which it is not half sufficient. If we consider this we shall be at no loss to account for the necessity of importation without supposing any decay in the state of agriculture. If we consider too the vastly increased consumption of finer food for man, and of corn for horses, to which our great wealth has given occasion, we shall see how a still greater quantity of corn is rendered necessary; and from all these circumstances we shall be forced to conclude that unless agriculture had made rapid advances during the period since the suspension of the bounty on exportation, a much greater importation must have been necessary than we have experienced.

But we need not pursue these comparisons. The advocates for the bounty admit all that is necessary for their own refutation. They do not pretend that agriculture has declined. They would only expose themselves to ridicule if they did. There are too many proofs that it has not declined for any one to dare to dispute it. These advocates therefore do not deny that so far from declining, agriculture is improving. I know not that there is one among them who will hesitate to admit that it has improved as fast during the last

50 years, as it did during the 50 years preceding. But whether they will admit this willingly or not, the fact is certain. And every document we have tends to prove that the augmentation of capital, of skill, and by consequence of produce in agriculture, has been much greater during the latter period than during the former. Agriculture, instead of declining, has advanced therefore since the suspension of the bounty, and has advanced more rapidly since it was suspended than before.

Observe then the admirable consistency of the advocates for the bounty. They say that this law greatly promoted agriculture, and that agriculture, suffered much when it was repealed; yet they allow that agriculture has been more rapidly improved since that law was repealed, than it was during the time when that law was in operation. An ordinary reasoner would think that a contrary conclusion were fully as reasonable ; that because agriculture has been more improved since the bounty law was repealed, therefore the bounty law was injurious to agriculture. Oh! but, say those ingenious speculators, we then could export corn, and we now must import it. What can be concluded from this but that we have more people to eat corn? They want however to bring the quantity of corn we raise on a level with the quanity of people we have to eat it; that is to say, they want to make agriculture increase as fast as commerce. So do I; and so does every one who understands and wishes well to the interests of his country. But is granting of a bounty on the ex-

portation of corn the way to do this? Certainly
not. Have we not shewn by the fact that commerce encreased as much faster than agriculture
while such a bounty existed, as it has done since
that bounty was taken away?

Their argument from experience then is altogether inconclusive, and fallacious.

CHAP. II.

Influence of the principle of Population upon the Corn Trade.

Beside the argument from experience, it was
stated that the advocates for a bounty on the exportation of corn pretend to conclude from the
nature of the case that this bounty is a beneficial
thing. This argument may be expressed as follows.
The bounty, they say, opens a large market
to the farmer; secures to him a reasonable profit;
thus encourages him to augment the produce of
his land; and so improves agriculture.

The whole strength of this argument evidently
depends upon the assumption, that without this
bounty a sufficient market would not exist for the
farmer. It is not enough that he enjoys the monopoly of the home market; it is not enough that
you allow him the market of the whole world in a
free exportation. You must pay him over and
above for carrying his corn to this foreign market.
But is this in reality the nature of the farmer's
business? It requires the examination only of a

single principle, a principle very well understood,
and indeed thus far not very difficult to understand, to see that the nature of the farmer's business is altogether different, and is in this respect
most remarkably distinguished from all other
trades.

It is very extraordinary that the persons who
have pretended to dictate laws on this subject have
never reflected that corn is a peculiar commodity;
that it has relations different from those of any
other commodity which man possesses; that these
are among the most important relations which are
found in that vast chain of connected things, on
which his being and animal nature depends; and
that the very elements of society are interwoven
with the laws which regulate the production of
this primary article.

No proposition is better established than this,
that the multiplication of the human species is always in proportion to the means of subsistence.
No proposition too is more incontrovertible than
this, that the tendency of the human species to
multiply is much greater than the rapidity with
which it seems possible to increase the produce of
the earth for their maintenance. For the full elu-
cidation of this proposition, if any one is capable
of doubting it, we refer to Mr. Malthus's ingenious book on the principle of population. No one
however will hesitate to allow all that is necessary
for our argument, that the tendency of the species
to multiply is much greater than the rapidity with

which there is any chance that the fruits of the earth will be multiplied in Britain, or any other country in Europe. What is the consequence of this great law of society, but that the production of corn creates the market for corn ? Raise corn as fast as you please, mouths are producing still faster to eat it. Population is invariably pressing close upon the heels of subsistence ; and in whatever quantity food be produced, a demand will always be produced still greater than the supply. The exportation of corn, therefore, is not so very simple a thing as the advocates for the bounty wish to make it appear. By checking population it produces at least one effect, which no wise politician will disregard.

We see then that the nature of this elementary principle of society, of which we never ought to lose sight, is such that a sufficient market is always provided at home, for all the corn which the land, with the utmost exertions of the farmer, can ever be made to produce , that the demand will always be proportioned to the supply, however great that supply may be ; and that a foreign market can never be wanted for any quantity of corn that can be regularly produced. A foreign market can never be necessary, but to take off the surplus of an extraordinary year. To send away any part of the regular produce of the country, however rapidly that produce may be increasing, is just to cut short a proportional part of the natural population of the country. That this ought not to be done but for very weighty reasons, surely needs no proof.

Two circumstances there are which alter this rule. In America, though population has increased so fast as to double itself every twenty years, a civilized people thinly scattered on a virgin soil have been able to increase the produce of the earth still faster than they have been able to multiply. This is a single instance in the history of the world. There is another circumstance of a different nature. When the natural tendency to multiply is checked by the vices of the government; when the wretched peasantry of a half-peopled country are in a great measure fed upon the spontaneous produce of the ground, and upon the cattle maintained on the waste lands, a great part of the little corn which is raised must be exported to nourish the pride of the great lords.

With the exception of these two cases I may lay it down as an incontrovertible proposition, that in every country an adequate demand, and even an urgent demand is always provided at home for the greatest possible increase of the fruits of the earth; and that the very principles of population ensure an ample encouragement to the utmost exertions of the farmer. From this proposition too it appears a very clear deduction, that in every well governed country, and whose circumstances are not as extraordinary as those of America, there never will be any *voluntary* exportation of corn, unless of the extraordinary produce of a

plentiful year; for that people will always be produced to consume at home the *regular* produce,
however rapidly it may increase.

This view of the subject seems altogether to
have escaped the advocates for the bounty. On
its importance however, it is surely unnecessary to
dwell. It is impossible that any thing affecting
so strongly one of the primary laws of society
should not be of the very first importance. If
then it follows from this important fact that an
ample market, and full encouragement is always
afforded to the farmer without the assistance of a
bounty, all, as far as I can conceive, that can,
after this, be said in defence of the bounty is,
that though the principle of population affords
sufficient encouragement to the raising of corn,
the bounty affords additional encouragement. Before entering into the merits of this point, I should
be inclined to say at first, that the over-doing of
a good thing never, in any case that I can remem-
ber, has been productive of beneficial effects.
Why, if a sufficient market is provided for corn,
and sufficient encouragement for its production,
should you interfere, and disturb the natural
course of things? But we will not be satisfied with
this general presumption against the bounty; a
presumption, however, in which there is no little
weight. By examining the particular circumstances of the case with a little attention, we shall
find that the advocates for the bounty have spoken
completely without thought, and without observ-

ing the most obvious circumstances, when they ascribed to the bounty the power of increasing the production of corn.

———————

CHAP. III.

Effects of the Bounty on the Rent of Land.

THE Intention of the bounty on the exportation of corn is to prevent the price of corn from ever falling so low as otherwise it would often naturally do. This either raises the average price of corn in the country, or it does not. The advocates for the bounty sometimes express themselves as if it did not ; for they are not very consistent with themselves on this point, sometimes endeavouring to recommend their doctrine by the popular promise of average cheapness ; though at other times it suits their argument to shew the opposite face of the subject. If the bounty however does not raise the average price of corn, it is impossible it can encourage the production. This is a proposition which I think I may save myself the trouble of proving. It is not the having a greater price than usual for a commodity one year, compensated by as great a deficiency the next, which tends to encourage the production of any commodity. It is the average profit on the trade which determines the value of the trade. A high average profit encourages it. A low average profit the contrary. If the bounty then lowers the average price of corn, it must of necessity discourage the raising of corn.

I believe, however, that the advocates for the bounty will easily give up this opinion. They will admit that the bounty raises to a certain degree the average price of corn. This high price they say would so encourage the raising of corn, that we should have a considerable quantity to export, which would bring us a good deal of money in all good years, and save us from scarcity in all bad ones. Let us consider how far these effects can be produced by the bounty. We only desire too the advocates to consider a very obvious principle. It is nothing but that common competition which regulates every trade, and of which it is astonishing that they should be so unable to perceive the effects. This high price of corn immediately raises the profit of farming stock and labour somewhat above the ordinary rate of profit in other employments. This as immediately creates a competition. The demand for farms becomes greater. The landlords are enabled to let their land higher, till farming profit comes again on a level with the profit of the general business of the country. Here then we are again in the very situation we were in before. Agriculture is a little more animated for a few years, till things find their proper level ; and then it returns exactly to the condition from which it set out. The value of land is somewhat raised ; and the price of corn has become higher; and these are the only effects. The first is an effect neither good nor bad, but as it is connected with the other; the last is one of the most unfortunate events that can befall any country. Nothing is more certain than that the landlords have it in their power to prevent the profits of the farmers from ever remaining any long time above the lowest, which is consistent with the nature of their business; that is, the rate common in the same country in other businesses equally agreeable. But surely no man in his senses can say that the farmer, if his profits are always the same, is in the smallest degree more encouraged when the price of corn is high than when it is low. The bounty then has no permanent influence to increase the production of corn. Its sole effect is to put money into the pockets of the proprietors of land, by taking it out of the pockets of all the other classes of the people; and to enrich a few present farmers who happen to have long leases; who will waste the ground with all their might to bring corn out of it, while these leases last; but will beware not to execute any expensive improvements, because they know they will be obliged to pay dearly for all their advantages, as soon as they have the lease to renew.

CHAP. IV.

Effects of the Bounty on the Profits of the Farmer.

WE have already seen that the contract which the landlord has to make with the farmer necessarily reduces the profit of the farmer to the very lowest consistent with the nature of his business ; whatever may be the price of the commodity which he raises. There is another circumstance which, independently of this contract, would speedily produce the same effect, and prevent any bounty whatever from contributing to the improvement of agriculture.

Those persons must be ignorant indeed, who need to be told that there is a balance of profits in all the different species of business carried on in any country. The per centage is not indeed exactly the same. Because some trades are less agreeable than others ; some have more risk ; and for those circumstances it is reasonable that a compensation should be made. But it is plain that reckoning all the agreeable, and all the disagreeable circumstances as profit or loss in every trade, there is an exact equality of profit in all the branches of free trade in any country. Any particular branch may obtain a temporary ascendency, but it is soon reduced by the influx of rivals in the trade, who naturally flock to the most gainful business.

According to this principle it is abundantly certain that the profits of the farmer must be upon this level before any bounty is applied in his favour, and must continue upon it, though no bounty were ever applied; and it is equally certain that no bounty can ever raise them above this level. Were they not upon this level, competitors would withdraw from the trade till they rose to it. Should they be raised ever so little above it, competitors would crowd into it till they brought them down.

Let us first suppose that a bounty is granted upon production. The farmer sold his corn before at the reasonable profit. If we suppose that he sells it at the same profit now, and gets the bounty over and above, his profit is raised much higher than that of all his countrymen in other trades. Some of them we may be assured will immediately endeavour to obtain a share of his high profits. New competitors cannot come into the same market without reducing the rate of profit; and this competition must continue till the rate of profit is brought down to the established and unalterable level. The business of agriculture is progressive during the period of this competition; but as soon as ever things are brought back to their natural state, and that is in a very short time, that business becomes stationary as before. To produce any permanent effects then by bounties on production, one bounty would not be sufficient; a new bounty would need to be im-

posed every four or five years; and by this progress
we might increase the price of wheat as rapidly as
we do the national debt. The absurdity of such
a measure as this is sufficiently exposed by the
very mention of it.

But the advocates for the bounty on exportation
may say, that the case is not the same with this,
as with the bounty on production. The foreign
market they may represent as so extensive that all
the competition which would be produced by the
greatest increase of British corn, could have very
little effect in reducing the price, and by consequence in reducing the profits of the British farmer.

Are we then to suppose it to be the opinion of
those persons, that they can raise the profits of the
farmer permanently above the profits of the other
species of business in the country? They may as
well undertake to procure for him sunshine and
rain whenever each would be agreeable. Every
removal of stock from the other kinds of business
in the country to that of farming lessens the competition of capital in all those kinds of business,
and thus raises the rate of profit. If the profit of
the farmer does not fall by this increase of capital,
more capital leaves the other trades of the country, and the profit in them rises, till at last they
are brought upon an equality with the business of
the farmer. The only effectual method, therefore, the only method by which in the nature of
things, the profits of the farmer can be raised

above the profits in other trades, is to erect the farmers into an exclusive corporation, like the East India Company, and to limit both the number of persons, and the quantity of capital which shall be employed in the trade. I wonder, if the advocates for the bounty will recommend this as a scheme for improving agriculture! They might by this means undoubtedly raise the profits of the farmers; because they might give just as little as they pleased to the landlords as rent, and demand just as much as they pleased from the people for corn. Without this or any other artificial scheme, the profits of the farmer are, and ever must be on an exact level, subject to the trifling fluctuations which belong to this as to all trades, with the rate of profit in the other species of business in the country.

This is so necessarily and obviously true, that it is surely a matter of surprise to find a committee of the House of Commons talk of its being necessary to make a law, (see Report from the Committee on the Corn Trade, ordered to be printed on the 14th of May, 1804, p. 4.) " to secure a certain and uniform, fair and reasonable price to the farmer." Why did they not recommend a law " to secure to him the certain and uniform birth of a fair and reasonable number" of calves and foals, from the number of cows and mares he employs as breeders? What insures the maker of knives and forks, or of ploughs and spades, a reasonable profit? Why, the market. Is not this sufficient to secure to every trader the profit which belongs to his business? Is it not absolutely necessary, by the very nature of things, that this should do so?

All those persons who are capable of estimating a statesman by the knowledge he displays of the genuine principles of national prosperity, will not forget the declaration of Mr. Pitt in the House of Commons, on a day when the price of wheat in Mark-lane was 70s. the quarter, " that the price of corn was not nearly high enough." This declaration was founded on one of the most vulgar of all vulgar prejudices; " that a high price of corn is useful to encourage the raising of corn;" a prejudice which we should suppose that, after a moment's reflection, no man of common sense could entertain. Who does not know that it is the profit of farming stock, which forms the encouragement of the farmer? And who does not know that the profit of farming stock may be as high, or higher, when corn is sold cheap as when it is sold dear? That therefore the encouragement of agriculture may be greater when the price of corn is low than when it is high? Is it found that the profit of other trades rises in proportion to the price of the article? So far from it, that the very reverse is in general found to be the case.

Mr. Burke, from whom it were to be wished that many of those, who have so well learned anti-jacobinism from him, would learn something else, has admirably observed in that Tract to which we have already alluded, "That a greater and more ruinous mistake cannot be fallen into, than that the trades of agriculture and of grazing can be conducted upon any other than the common principles of commerce."—"The balance between consumption and production," says he," makes price. The market settles, and alone can settle that price. Nobody, I believe, has observed with any reflection what market is, without being astonished at the truth, the correctness, the celerity, the general equity with which the balance of things is settled. Talking of the profit of the farmer, he says, "Who are to judge what that profit and advantage ought to be? Certainly, no authority on earth. It is a matter of convention, dictated by the reciprocal conveniences of the parties, and indeed by their reciprocal necessities."

CHAP. V.

Effects of the Bounty on the Value of Silver.

I HAVE now shewn that there are two different circumstances; the power of the landlord to raise his rent, and the natural and unavoidable migration of capital; either of which is perfectly sufficient to prevent the profits of the farmer from ever being raised for any continuance of time, above the lowest consistent with the nature of the business; and that as the operation of both must

be united against the bounty, its effects with regard to agriculture must soon be terminated. It
is surely unnecessary to repeat the conclusion, that
if the profits of the farmer are not raised by the
bounty, it is impossible his encouragement to en-
large his business can be increased. What is the
reason, according to the zealots of this sect, which
renders the bounty necessary? Why, the insuf-
ficiency of the profits of the farmer. But the
bounty, it is now apparent, cannot alter those
profits. Therefore the bounty has no tendency
to produce the effect proposed by the advocates
for that measure.

But though the bounty produces no good effects,
it is not altogether without effects. We must next
advert to the view which Dr. Smith has exhibited
of this subject, a view which any one can affect
to treat lightly only from not understanding it. No
proposition is established more thoroughly to the
conviction of those who have studied the scientific
principles of political economy than this; that the
money price of corn, regulates the money price of
every thing else. The wages of the common labourer may in general be reckoned his maintenance.
He must earn a sufficient quantity of corn to feed
himself, otherwise he cannot exist. If he is paid in
money, the sum of money he daily receives must
always be equivalent to the quantity of corn he must
use. If the price of the corn is high he must receive
the greater sum of money, as his day's wages, to
buy it with. This is so obviously necessary, that

we need spend no more time in proving it. The money price of labour therefore is entirely regulated by the money price of corn.

Let us next see how the money price of corn affects that of every thing else. It is evident that it must regulate the price of all other products of the earth, as the culture of corn will encroach upon them till they become equally profitable with itself. " It regulates, for example," says Smith, " the money price of grass and hay, of butcher's meat, of horses, and the maintenance of horses, of land carriage consequently, or of the greater part of the inland commerce of the country."

All the commodities of any country consist either of the rude produce of the land, or of manufactured goods. We have seen that the money price of the rude produce of land is altogether determined by the money price of corn. The price of manufactured goods may be resolved into three parts ; 1st, The price of the raw material ; 2d, The wages of labour; 3d, The profit of stock. The money price of the first two, we have already seen, is altogether regulated by that of corn.

The quantity of circulating stock in every manufacture is in proportion to the value of the raw material, and the wages of the manufacturer. But we have seen that the price both of the raw material, and the wages of the labourer in all manufactures, are raised in exact proportion to the price of corn. More circulating capital, there-

fore, is wanted in that proportion to carry on
every manufacture, and the reasonable profit upon
this additional capital must be added to the price
of the manufactured commodity. Every one of
the three constituent parts of the price of all manufactured commodities receives then an increase
by every increase in the price of corn ; and thus
the price of all manufactured commodities must
rise in a much greater proportion than the price of
corn. The price therefore of labour, and of
every thing which is the produce of land and labour, every exchangeable commodity which the
country produces, is altogether determined by the
price of corn.

Nothing then can be more incontrovertible
than the proposition of Smith, that " the real
effect of the bounty is not so much to raise the
real value of corn, as to degrade the real value of
silver; or to make an equal quantity of it exchange for a smaller quantity, not only of corn,
but of all other commodities."

Two conclusions, therefore, evidently follow ;
The first is, that no ability whatever is by the
bounty procured to the farmer of increasing the
quantity of corn to be raised. " Though in consequence of the bounty," says Smith, " the farmer should be enabled to sell his corn for four
shillings the bushel instead of three and sixpence,
and to pay his landlord a money rent proportion-
able to this rise in the money price of his produce ; yet, if in consequence of this rise in the

price of corn, four shillings will purchase no more goods of any other kind than three and sixpence would have done before, neither the circumstances of the farmer, nor those of the landlord, will be in the smallest degree mended by this change. The farmer will not be able to cultivate better: the landlord will not be able to live better."

The second conclusion is, that in a country situated as ours at present is, in which so many complaints have been lately heard of the depreciation of money, produced by various causes, it surpasses the common measure of folly to enact a law more powerful to produce the evil, than any other cause which exists. This is a point which deserves the most serious consideration of every thinking man, and more particularly of every commercial man in the country. We have heard Mr. Pitt declare in the house of commons, when he was urging at the end of the last session of parliament an addition to the civil list money of the king, that the depreciation of money in this country had been not less than 60 or 70 per cent. within the last 30 or 40 years. This is enormous. Nothing similar to this has happened in the rest of Europe. What a prodigious disadvantage must not this lay us under in our commerce with all other countries? If we are still able to send goods to those countries, how much more should we be able to send, were this prodigious burthen removed, and we were able to sell our goods 60 per cent. cheaper? What is it that in such peculiar

circumstances we think proper to do? Why, to
add a new cause to increase the evil, a cause more
fundamental and more powerful than any which
previously existed. It behoves us to think a little
what we are about. The burthen may be increased
till our commerce can bear it no longer. Who
knows how soon a favourable turn may be produced in the unhappy affairs of the continent of
Europe, when we could not long support the bur-
thens which we at present bear? At a time when
our enormous taxation, the stoppage of payment
at the bank, and the vast expenditure of a war are
all operating to depreciate money in this country,
to urge an act to grant a bounty on the exportation of corn, which must lead so powerfully to
a still greater depreciation, betrays a criminal neg-
lect or ignorance of the best interests of the country, which deserves the utmost reprobation of this
age and of posterity.

We supposed that it was a proposition completely agreed upon by those who had studied the
principles of national wealth, and a proposition
which no one, bearing the name of a politician,
was ignorant of, that one of the most favourable,
and advantageous of all circumstances to a manufacturing country, was the cheapness of provisions. This determines the price of the raw material; it determines also the wages of the labourer; it determines therefore the price of the
manufacture. When this costs little at home, it
can be sold with great advantage abroad; it over-

comes all competition ; and the greatest quantity of it may be disposed of. When the price of corn on the other hand is high, this raises the price of the raw material of all manufactures, of the labour employed in them, and by consequence of the manufactured commodity; it must be sold dearer therefore abroad ; and by consequence less of it can be disposed of. How wonderfully circumscribed the range of reflection which dictates the arguments of those who defend the bounty ! They boast highly of the riches brought into the country by the annual exportation of a few hundred thousand quarters of corn, worth not so much as a million of money ; while manufactures to the value of many millions are by that means prevented from being exported ; while too the exportation of the corn has to be assisted by money which government pays, whereas the manufactures on the other hand would pay to government a large sum as duty ; and while, at the same time, all the corn exported would be consumed at home at a full price, in the preparation of those additional manufactures ; and by consequence the very same encouragement afforded to the farmer to prosecute his important business, as could have been by the exportation of his produce.

It is astonishing what a different course of reasoning men often pursue on subjects exactly similar, without being able to perceive their own inconsistency. On running over in one's mind some

of the acts of the British legislature, how many
cases does one find where it has acted on a principle directly the reverse of that on which it established the bounty law ; cases which are as vehemently applauded by the common tribe of politicians, as the bounty law itself! Why should wool,
for example, have been always subject to a system
of laws, absolutely and immediately contradictory
to the principle of the corn bounty ? Why, if a
bounty on the exportation of corn be so favourable to the production of corn, should not a
bounty on the exportation of wool be favourable
to the production of wool ? Why, if the exportation of corn have such an effect to produce
plenty of corn at home, should not the exportation of wool have an effect to produce plenty of
wool at home ? How has it been, that while the
legislature has so often encouraged the exportation
of corn, it has always prohibited the exportation
of wool with so much anxiety, and punished it
with so much severity ? Why are such inconsis-
tencies still allowed to disgrace the intellects of our
law-givers ? What difference can be pointed out
between the case of wool and that of corn ? If it
be said that we have not wool enough to answer
our occasions, neither have we corn enough. If
it be said that wool is the material of one of our
most important manufactures ; corn is the most
important material of all our manufactures. If it
be of importance that the raw material of any of

our manufactures should be got cheap, surely it is of importance that what is the great material of them all should be got cheap.

Why, if granting a bounty on exportation be so effectual a means of producing plenty and creating riches, do we not establish a bounty on the exportation of gold and silver ? Why do we not grant a bounty on the exportation of sheep and oxen, butter and cheese, ale, porter, and spirits ? Why not on tables and chairs, and all other articles of furniture ? Nay, to go higher, why, in order to increase population, not grant a bounty on the exportation of men and women ? Why not, especially, grant a bounty on the exportation of such classes as we have most need of, soldiers, for example, and sailors ; As for politicians, we have such a supply of them, the very best in their kind, that we have no occasion for exportation, unless it be as a security against any decay in the numbers or breed.

We know of no person who has pretended to point out any defect in this argument of Dr. Smith; except a Mr. Mackie, who calls himself a farmer in East Lothian, in Scotland, and who has published two letters in the same volume with the performance of Mr. Dirom. The gross ignorance which those letters betray of some of the most important, and best established principles of the important subject on which the author has treated, might have exempted me from the task of exposing the futility of his objections, if it did not

appear that conclusions, similar to those of Mr.
Mackie, whether drawn from the same premises
or not, are both adopted, and important regula-
tions founded upon them for conducting the business of the nation. Let us hear to what extent Mr.
Mackie's objections reach. There are three different states in which Dr. Smith says the affairs of
all countries may be considered as placed, the
declining, stationary, or advancing states. In the
first two of these, Mr. Mackie allows that the
ideas of Dr. Smith hold completely, but denies
that they do so in the third. " I readily," says
he, p. 319, " agree that the money price of corn
may produce this effect (regulate the money price
of all things) in a nation where the state of society is stationary or declining; such as China or
Hindostan; but when applied to Britain, or any
country advancing in wealth and population, the
argument appears to me to be unfounded." Mr.
Mackie is one of that class of authors from whom
you cannot get any precise account of the grounds
of their opinions, who throw down a number of
circumstances more or less remotely connected
with the point in question, then assert the
conclusion which they wish to draw, and leave
you to find the connection between it and the
premises the best way you can.

The most distinct statement of the reasons for
his dissent from the conclusions of Smith, which I
have found in the letter, is in these words, p. 221 :
" But in countries where industry, population, and

wealth, going on in a progressive state of improvement, are constantly encreasing the national capital, and continually adding to the general consumption, *these causes* alone operate to raise the money price of labour and every other commodity, without being in the smallest degree affected by the money price of corn." What *causes* does the author mean? Does he mean an increasing state of industry, population, and wealth; or certain effects which he mentions of these increasing circumstances, namely, an augmentation of capital and an augmentation of consumption? As far as we can gather his meaning from his various details it is this last. An increase of industry, population and wealth produces an increase of capital and an increase of consumption; and an increase of. capital and of consumption produces an increase in the price of labour and of commodities. In a country in this progressive state these causes *alone* he says produce this increase of wages and price, " without being in the smallest degree affected by the money price of corn." Here the grammatical construction of the author's language bears that the *causes* he mentions, the increase of capital and of consumption, are not in the smallest degree affected by the money price of corn; but as this is nonsense, or at least altogether foreign to the purpose, we may suppose he means to say, if he knew how to express himself, that it is the " price of labour and of every other commodity," which is not in the smallest degree affected by the money price of corn. Now if this be so ; it is something very strange. When a country is in a declining or a stationary condition, two out of the three possible conditions, a rise in the price of corn, even according to this author himself, necessarily produces a rise in the price of labour, and of every other commodity, but as soon as ever a country begins to go forward a rise in the price of corn loses all this power; and the increase of capital and of consumption prevents it from having any effect whatever upon the price of labour and commodities. What a wonderful thing this increase of capital and of consumption must be ? Why does not some adept in the science of political economy undertake to prove, (it would be a task admirably suitable to the talents of Mr. Mackie,) that a rotation of crops is a thing very serviceable to increase the productive power of land in the declining and stationary states of a country, but loses all this efficacy in the advancing state ?

I wonder if Mr. Mackie means to assert that a rise in the price of corn has no effect in the advancing state of a country upon the other species of the rude produce of the earth; upon the price of potatoes, for example, or hay, or flax ? Or if he supposes that a farmer, who knew he would make more by sowing corn in his field than any of those articles, would not sow corn instead of them, and every other farmer the same, till the quantity of those articles would become so diminished as to raise their price to a level with that of corn. Because if Mr. Mackie knows not this principle, or is incapable of perceiving its validity, I cannot descend to instruct him; I write for others than him. Here is one large class of articles then undoubtedly affected by the money price of corn; and raised in price in the same proportion exactly. There is another large class of articles of which those form the raw materials. So far therefore as the price of the raw material enters into the price of those articles, so far is their price also affected by that of corn. So far too as an increase in the price of the raw material requires an additional quantity of capital to carry on the same quantity of business, and by consequence an additional profit upon that additional capital, so far is the price of those articles still farther affected by the price of corn.

The absurdity of the assertion with regard to labour is almost equally obvious. When a country is stationary the wages of the labourer are sufficient to maintain him, and to preserve the number of labourers from decreasing, and no more. In this state of things the author allows, and it is very certian, whether he allows it or not, that every increase in the money price of the article by which the labourer is maintained must be accompanied by a correspondent rise in his wages. This rise however is merely nominal. The reward of his labour, the quantity of maintenance which he can command is the same as ever. It is the money price, therefore, Smith says, and not the real price which is affected by the money price of corn. When from this state a country begins to advance, the demand for labour increases ; those who want to employ it bid against one another ; and the wages of labour rise. This is an increase in the real price of labour, in the quantity of maintenance which the labourer can command. It is in general, however, a rise in the money price at the same time. The fluctuations in the value of money are in general slow, and the changes in the course of a few years are scarcely perceptible. If we suppose then that the prosperity of Great Britain, for example, and the demand for labour should increase so fast as to raise the price of labour one third in the course of five years, the value of money remaining all this while the same, the rise in the money price, and the rise in the real price of labour would be the same. The quantity of money which the labourer would receive would be one third greater ; and the quantity of maintenance which he could command would likewise be one third greater. Now observe the proposition of Mr. Mackie. This increasing demand for labour, he says, has a tendency to raise the money price of labour only, not the real ; a proposition than which a more senseless was probably never set down upon paper. Though the price of the labourer's mantenance, says he, be so raised during this time, that one third more of money will be able to purchase no more than might have been purchased by one third less at the beginning of

that period, the wages of the labourer will be only
raised one third in money. They will not be raised
in the smallest degree in reality. The quantity of
maintenance which he can command will still be
the same, that is the lowest capable of preserving
the number of labourers from being reduced by
starvation. But if any one is capable of supposing that a growing demand for labour, capable of
raising the real price of labour one third, can be
prevented from raising that price at all, only by a
rise in the price of provisions, I do not think it
necessary to spend time to instruct him.

The whole of this miserable attempt has been
produced by the incapacity of the author to attend
to the distinction between the money price and
the real price of labour. Whoever is capable of
understanding the effects of prosperity, that is of
a growing demand for labour upon the price
of labour, must see that is produces effects
upon the real price of labour, that is upon the
quantity of maintenance which the labourer can
command. If therefore the money price of that
maintenance has risen one third while the rate of
his wages has risen one third, the money price of
his labour must have risen not one third only but
two thirds; " nothing" says Mr. Burke (Thoughts
and Details on Scarcity) " is such an enemy to ac-
curacy of judgment as a coarse discrimination."

It is unnecessary to pursue this subject any farther. It now appears that the money price of all
the raw materials produced in the country, and also

that the money price of labour are altogether determined by the money price of corn. I have already
shewn in what manner a rise in the price of the
material, and of the labour, requires an additional
capital in every species of manufacture, and an
additional profit upon that capital. The rise then
on all the component parts, into which the price
of commodities can be divided, is exactly the
same in the advancing as in all the other states of
society. It therefore clearly appears that uni-
versally the money price of corn regulates the
money price of every thing else; and by consequence that " the real effect of the bounty,"
to repeat the language of Smith, " is not so much
to raise the real value of corn, as to degrade the
real value of silver, or to make an equal quantity
of it exchange for a smaller quantity, not only of
corn, but of all other commodities."

I flatter myself that I have now fully proved
that a bounty on the exportation of corn, never
has had any effect, and never can have any, to
encourage the cultivation of corn, or to increase
the quantity of it produced. Every possible plea
then for the policy of granting the bounty is taken
away. I have proved, too, that the high price of
corn to which the bounty is intended to give occasion, while it has no tendency whatever to encourage agriculture, has a necessary tendency to
discourage every other species of industry, and to
produce the greatest evils. I have therefore exhibited the strongest reasons for the speedy repeal
of the corn law which was passed at the end of the

last session of parliament. I am happy to understand that it is in the contemplation of many of the most respectable bodies of men in the kingdom, to petition parliament for the repeal of that law as soon after it meets as possible. They cannot attend to a concern which more strongly affects their own interest, as well as the interest of the nation at large; and it is eagerly to be hoped that they will be joined by all other bodies of a similar description. In that case no doubt whatever need be entertained of the immediate repeal of this statute. The British Parliament wants only the due information to be laid before it, in such a manner as to bear down the influence of ignorance and private interest. On its integrity and patriotism, as a body, the public relies, as it has every reason to rely, with the most perfect confidence.

In reading the different publications in which that measure is recommended, I have been struck, as I think every well informed person will be struck, with the total want of all general views, by which their authors are distinguished. They strongly betray a most limited acquaintance with the great principles of political philosophy. They take up a single particular; they are vehemently struck with one peculiar aspect which it shews; but are unable to extend their view to all the parts of the great subject with which it is connected; and are thus perpetually deceived in their reasonings and conclusions. The mistakes of

such men might easily be overlooked, even their
vanity and presumption might be pardoned, if we
did not so often find that their partial, and con-
tracted views adapt themselves to the understand-
ings of men who have the power to carry their
follies into execution, and thus become the principles upon which the affairs of nations are conducted, and by which the happiness of millions is
determined.

CHAP. VI.

Exportation.

BUT though a bounty on exportation is
thus clearly ineffectual to encourage agriculture,
and thus particularly calculated to discourage
every other branch of industry, and to produce
the greatest mischief to the nation; a free exportation appears by no means to deserve the
same condemnation. In the first place, " to hinder the farmer," says Smith, whose language we
are always happy to use on every subject of which
he has treated, " from sending his goods at all
times to the best market, is evidently to sacrifice
the ordinary laws of justice, to an idea of public
utility, to a sort of reasons of state; an act of legi-
slative authority which ought to be exercised only,
which can be pardoned only, in cases of the most
urgent necessity." It is evident that to subject
the commerce of grain to any forced conditions

may naturally be expected to have effects very dif
ferent from those produced by the free, natural,
unrestrained course of the trade; that while the
one may be expected to be altogether salutary,
the other may be suspected to be very prejudicial.

The effects, however, of an absolute prohibition
of the exportation of grain, would be far different
from those which are generally supposed, and from
those which are held forth by those gentlemen of
long views, who preach abroad the doctrine of the
bounty on exportation.

It would have no effect whatever to discourage
agriculture. It is abundantly evident from the
principle of population, that to whatever height the
general and medium produce of the land could
be brought up, new inhabitants would be produced
to consume it, and to give for it an equivalent.

For this medium produce there will always be a
competent market, and a competent demand in
the home consumption, the surplus produce of an
extraordinarily plentiful year, would however re-
gorge. That is never more than sufficient to
make up for the deficiency of unfavourable years.
However, during the plentiful years, though part
of the surplus produce would be reserved to supply this deficiency of the years of scarcity; part
would no doubt come into the market, and reduce the price. That part again which was reserved for the years of scarcity would hinder the
price from rising so high as then it would
otherwise do. By this means the price of corn

would be at all times somewhat lower that if exportation were permitted. But what would be the consequence to the farmer? Why the landlord would be obliged to let his land cheaper, and the profits of the farmer would remain the same. It is evident that the natural migration of capital would infallibly produce this effect. But if the profits of the farmer remain the same, the encouragement of his business would remain also the same. What too would be the consequence to the landlord? Neither would he be a loser. The low price of corn would reduce the price of labour and of every thing else ; he would find himself just as rich as he was before. He would be able to hire the same number of servants, to build as magnificent a house, to buy as many articles, either of necessity or of luxury as he did before.

What, in the next place, would be the effects of a free exportation? I have already established as an undeniable proposition, that in every country, in ordinary circumstances, where the principle of population is not checked by the vices of the government, no part of the medium produce of grain will ever be exported, but in consequence of some forced regulation. According to this proposition it is only the surplus of an extraordinary year that can go out of the country by a free exportation. Now it is abundantly evident that whatever quantity of corn is exported in those favourable years, an equal quantity must be imported in unfavourable years. There is by the supposition, a sufficient number of people in the country to consume the whole produce of a medium year; therefore you cannot, by your exportation in a plentiful year, reduce the quantity of corn in the country below that medium produce, without destroying some of your people by hunger; and you must bring the produce of a scanty year up to that medium by importation, or you must allow some of your people to perish in this case too, from hunger.

What then would be the effects of these operations upon prices and produce ? It is evident that the exportation of a plentiful year could not raise the price above that of a medium year ; because it is the high price of a medium year, and the great demand at home, which prevents any part of that produce from going abroad. The importation in a scanty year would bring the price upon a level with the general free market, common to all the nations of the world, which would always be the same, or nearly the same, with the medium price at home. By this process the price of corn is preserved at all times very near that rate, which an exact proportion between the produce of the country, and the inhabitants of the country requires; a rate, and a process, which, by consequence, have, beyond all contrivances, the most powerful effect to produce that exact proportion. The progress of agriculture too, its gradual improvement, is, in this case, left to the impulse of the general circumstances of the country, to that powerful tendency in population to multiply, as fast as the circumstances of the country will permit.

It is easy to see in what manner this beautiful process is disturbed by the application of bounties. In the first place a bounty upon exportation carries more corn out of the country in the good years, than would go of its own accord. And in the next place, a bounty upon importation in bad years, brings more corn into the country than would come of its own accord. In the one case, we send abroad more corn than we can spare; and in the other, we bring home more than we have any occasion for. There is a direct loss of double freight, insurance, and profit, upon all that corn which is exported, only to be brought back again, and imported only to be sent out again. But this is the least part of the evil. By the one operation we produce for a time a much higher price, than would otherwise be produced, and a proportionate part of the miseries of scarcity: By the other, we produce a much lower price than would otherwise be produced. We thus maintain a perpetual fluctuation, and all the inconveniencies and miseries which violent fluctuation produces both to the farmer and to the people.

To the persons who plead even for a forced exportation, we need adduce no more in favour of a free exportation. But there are persons, and those too, of considerable profundity in the science of political economy, who think that the export-

ation of corn ought to be altogether prohibited.
If we prohibit the exportation without permitting
importation, the effects will be as follows. It is
impossible so to preserve the surplus produce of
the good years, as to make it compensate the deficiency of the bad. Part of it will find its way
into the market in the good years, and be wasted
and consumed. This part will be wanting for the
supply of the bad years, and produce all the hardships of great scarcity. By this process too, the
most violent fluctuation in prices, must be produced; as the surplus in the market must sink
them very low in the good years, and the incur-
able deficiency raise them enormously high in the
bad.

If we prohibit exportation, but allow importation, the deficiency left by the extravagant consumption and waste of the good years, remains
always to be supplied by importation during the
bad. This is a policy, therefore, directly calculated to render the average production of the
country always inadequate to the consumption of
the country. It is a policy, too, calculated to produce very great fluctuation; though not altogether
so great as the non-importation scheme. The part
of the surplus produce, which, during the good
years finds its way into the market, must be, much
greater than under that scheme; since nobody
will have nearly so great a motive to reserve it.
The depreciation of prices, therefore, will be much
greater. Importation, will, indeed, prevent the

prices in the bad years from rising so high. But the expence of freight and insurance must render the imported corn considerably above the rate of medium years, and therefore very greatly above the enormously reduced prices of the years of great plenty.

CHAP. VII.

Importation.

THE sect who admire the duty on exportation, are terribly afraid of a free importation. They desire to confine importation within the narrowest limits, and indeed to permit it at all, only in cases of the greatest necessity. Their prejudices are miserable. It would, they say, ruin the farmer, and hurt agriculture.

There is only one direct effect, which a free importation can produce ; that is, a reduction of the average price of corn. I have already stated reasons to prove that this reduction would have no tendency to reduce the profits of the farmers, nor to injure agriculture. Even the single argument of Smith, Mr. Mackie, the most dauntless champion of the monopoly system, allows, would be perfectly adequate to support this conclusion, if it held as truly in the advancing state, as it does in the declining or stationary states of society. I have proved that it does hold in that state as well as in both the others. It is therefore extorted from this eager adversary, that the importation can have no bad effects.

But it may be necessary, though not for the refutation of my opponents, for the satisfaction of the public, to consider a little more minutely the effects of a free importation.

It is evident that the market from which all corn imported must be brought, is the general free market, common to all countries in the world. Now, as the domestic market in every country is regulated by the wants and superfluities of the individuals who inhabit the country ; so this general market of all countries is regulated by the wants and superfluities of the different countries which repair to it. It is the nature of this market to be very stationary, and scarcely subject at all to fluctuation. For though one country may very much fail in a particular year, or very much abound, that is never the case with all countries ; and the deficiency of one or more is always very exactly supplied by the super-abundance of others ; so that a steady medium price is always maintained in this market of nations.

The adversaries of a free importation tell us that countries, such as North America, Poland, and the countries around the Baltic, which are thinly peopled, and in which manufactures are but little established, can always raise corn cheaper than fully peopled, rich, and commercial countries ; and that if importation is permitted from those countries free, they must undersell our farmers greatly, and so ruin agriculture. Those persons understand not, in the least degree, the nature of that great general market, in which the wants of all nations are supplied. We are not competitors in that market with poor nations only, but with rich also, with all the nations in the world. It is the circumstances therefore of all the richest nations, of those who are most completely our rivals, which settle the price in that market; and we are forced to buy in it not according to the circumstances of the poor nation, but according to those of the rich.

Corn never can be bought for importation into Great Britain below that standard price, in the market of nations, which is established by the wants and superfluities of them all; and which therefore must be the medium price of the nations which come into that market, taken altogether. The medium in some of them may be above it; and the medium in others below. These are the two extremes. But in all the rest it must be nearly the same. Whatever corn, therefore, is at any time imported into Great Britain must come into it purchased at this medium price, and loaded with all the expence of freight and insurance from the country where it is bought. And corn is an article of so much bulk in proportion to the value, that this expence must always bear a pretty high proportion to the original price. Foreign corn, therefore, can never come into England very cheap; and unless in England the medium price

of corn be very much above the medium price in
the other countries of Europe, none can ever be
imported, except in years of particular scarcity.
If the medium price in England therefore be the
same with the standard of the universal market,
which there is good reason to think it is, agriculture cannot receive any discouragement from a free
importation, even on the principles of the bounty
people themselves.

But let us suppose that the medium price in
England is very much above this standard. This
must be owing either to some peculiar degrada-
tion of the value of money in England, an evil of
the greatest magnitude, and which the free importation of corn would greatly tend to redress,
and without affecting permanently, or to any considerable degree, either the profits of the farmer,
or the interests of agriculture. Or if the value of
money be the same in England as it generally is in
the rest of Europe, and the medium price of corn
be still higher, it must be owing to this, that a
smaller proportion of the people are engaged in
agriculture, and a greater in other occupations.
Now this must arise from one or other of two
causes, either from agriculture's being more encouraged in those countries, or from other occupations having more encouragement in this country. In almost all the countries of Europe, the
same or greater discouragements are laid upon
agriculture than are laid in England. But in no
country in the world are there such encourage-

ments to other occupations. England then has the same advantage with regard to agriculture as other nations, but advantages peculiar to herself with regard to other occupations. But it is always the wisdom of nations as well as of individuals to pursue the employments in which they have peculiar advantages, rather than others in which they have no advantages. With regard to the inconvenience of depending upon the great general market of nations for any part of our supply, it is to a nation with half the commerce, and naval resources of this country absolutely nothing at all. Nothing in human affairs can be more certainly depended upon than that market.

But if it be accounted an indispensable policy to bring the number of persons employed in agriculture, and those in other occupations to the proportion that the former shall at all times feed the latter, it must be done either by affording greater encouragements to agriculture, or imposing discouragements upon other occupations. The former will be the plan adopted undoubtedly. But to grant a bounty upon exportation, and to impose a duty upon importation, is to adopt the latter plan, not the former; is to discourage all foreign commerce, but to afford no encouragement whatever to agriculture, as we have already abundantly proved. To obtain this object then some other means must be devised of encouraging agriculture. And some most important ones are not far to seek. Render the commerce of land as free and easy as that of all things else; relieve agriculture from those vexatious imposts from which other occupations are exempted; and render the employment of large capital as independent in agriculture, and a source of as great authority, as it is in trade, and you will have no occasion to complain of a slowly progressive agriculture.

If importation is rendered free, so long as the price of corn in England is high enough to surpass the price in that general market of nations, together with all the expence of carriage into England, corn will flow into that country, till it reduce the price there to that in the general market, augmented by all this expence of carriage. If exportation is rendered free, as soon as corn in England sinks below the price in the general market, it will flow out of England till the price become as high as in that market, bating the expence of carriage. The medium price in England is thus rendered the same with the standard price in the general market; and the range of fluctuation is rendered very small indeed. Price can only depart from the medium by the expence of carriage added in the one case and subtracted in the other. That this steadiness and uniformity would be one of the most advantageous things both to the farmer and to every other class of the people, is too obvious to require any proof.

What now would be the effects of this reduction of price upon the general wealth of the country, and upon the progress of agriculture? It is evi-

dent that every country, in which the price of grain
is above the standard of this general market,
lies under peculiar disadvantages in respect of its
whole foreign commerce. The value of its money
is degraded below that of other countries exactly in
the same proportion; and to this extent it must be
undersold by other nations in all foreign markets.
To bring the price of grain therefore down to the
standard of the general market, is of the utmost
possible importance to foreign commerce, and to
all those interests of the state which are dependent
upon foreign commerce. What again would be the
effect of the same reduction upon the progress of
agriculture is abundantly evident from what has already been said. The owners of land would be obliged to reduce their rents till the farmers could
make the same profits as are usual in the country,
that is to say, the very same which they made before,
and by which, of course, they would have the very
same encouragement to improve their business. At
the same time neither the farmers nor the landlords
would be losers. The prices of every thing would
fall. And though they would not pay for the
things which they want with so much money, they
would be able to buy just as many as they were
before.

It may be shewn at the same time that the reduction of price in England by a free importation
would be very immaterial. This is of no consequence with regard to the real policy of the measure which we recommend. But it may serve to

render some persons who cannot regard it with the eye of a true statesman, less obstinate in their prejudices against it. Notwithstanding all that has been said about the deficiency of England in corn, it is abundantly certain that the medium price in England is very nearly the same with the standard price in the general market. This has undoubtedly been the opinion of the legislature as often as it granted a bounty on importation on the appearance of scarcity; because if the medium price were much above the general market, and that inhanced too by the appearance of scarcity, assuredly corn enough would come into the country without any bounty. As the bounty itself has never brought it with any peculiar rapidity, it is a certain proof that the price in England has never been very much above the general price in Europe.

The same thing appears from the state of the exportation of corn. Since the year 1790, the affairs of Europe have been so much deranged, and so many peculiar causes have affected the corn trade in England, that it would be unfair to draw any general conclusions from that period. From the year 1770 to the year 1790, we find that exportation and importation have alternated. During one year we have exported, during another we have imported. During the one year it is plain the price in England must have been below that in the general market, and during the other above it. The number of years however in

which it was above it is greater than that in which
it was below it. The price in England therefore
was during that period more frequently above the
price in the general market than below it. But it
was frequently below it; and therefore though the
medium price in England must have been somewhat above the standard price in the general market, it cannot have been much above it. The
same thing appears from another fact. Even in
the years of greatest importation, and when the
price by consequence must have been highest, we
always exported too. But this it is impossible we
could have done, had the price been much higher
in England than it was abroad. The same thing
appears too from the very small quantity of grain
imported during that period, notwithstanding the
rout which has been made about it. My readers
will perhaps be surprised when I tell them that of
the two most important species of grain, wheat and
barley, we have upon the whole of that period
exported more than we have imported to the
amount of 157,542 quarters; and it is altogether in the coarser species of grain, oats, pease,
and beans, that the extra importation has been
made.

From these considerations it evidently appears,
that by a free exportation and importation of corn,
the medium price in England would be somewhat
reduced, but not much; that this reduction would
be of the greatest importance to the country in

respect to its foreign trade, and no discouragement
whatever to agriculture ; and that this free trade
would produce a steady, regular price, very little
subject to fluctuation, which would preserve the
farmer from all the hardships of very low prices,
and the people from all the hardships of very high
prices ; that the system of bounties on the other
hand must raise the price of corn, which lays the
country under great disadvantage in respect to
foreign trade, without affording the smallest encouragement to agriculture ; and that it has a tendency to produce the greatest fluctuation in prices,
and to produce all the miseries and inconveniences
both of too high and of too low prices.

CHAP. VIII.

Landlords, Farmers, and Corn-dealers.

IT would not have been necessary for the present
purpose, to say any thing on this subject, were it
not on account of a prejudice which turns the attention of many people from the real object of
importance. As soon as ever prices are considerably raised, we immediately hear an outcry against
landlords, farmers, and corn-dealers. Nothing
can be more unjust, and at the same time of worse
consequence. High prices are never owing to

those orders of men, and never can be, unless we
make absurd laws, which force them into an unnatural situation. It is natural for the farmer and
for the corn-dealer to sell their commodity when
they can get the best price for it, and to keep it
when they expect that the price will rise. Every
other person, who has any thing to sell, does the
same thing; and it would be the utmost injustice
to refuse that liberty to the man who has corn to
sell. It would be the utmost folly too, as it
would soon reduce the quantity to be sold.

I need not repeat the proof which has been
produced by Smith, and is so generally understood that the interest of the farmer, and of the
corn-merchant is injured by any attempt to raise
the price higher than the supply requires ; and
that at all times when the trade in corn is free, the
interests of the traders in corn, and those of the
people at large, are exactly the same.

When it is so contrary therefore to all justice
and sense, to accuse the corn-dealers for any excess in the price of that article, it is truly provok-
ing to hear it continually charged upon them ; to
observe the attention of the country turned from
a true to a false cause of the evil, and the re-
medy by consequence perpetually missed.

On occasion of the present high prices, accordingly, the newspapers have all been loud, as usual,
against the corn-dealers ; and have endeavoured
by this vulgar cry, to turn the indignation of the

ignorant people, against an innocent, and most useful set of men, and to withdraw our attention from the operation of that bill which has lately passed.

After stating an argument of the same kind on this very subject, Mr. Burke expresses himself thus severely against those publications, which are contributing powerfully to corrupt both our public taste and public spirit. " The consideration," says he, " of this ought to bind us all, rich and poor together, against those wicked writers of the newspapers, who would inflame the poor against their friends, guardians, patrons, and protectors."

Neither are the landlords to be blamed for making of their property as much as they can. Every other class of persons in the kingdom does the same ; and it is unjust to require greater sacrifices of them than of others. Neither can they be accused of generally besieging the legislature for laws, to favour their peculiar interests. Many other classes of men have been far more industrious in this respect than they. I am even persuaded were they once convinced that the late corn law is prejudicial to the interest of the country, that they would be the first to petition for its repeal. I am not without hopes that the preceding considerations will have weight with many of them. But I am too well aware of the hold which a favourite system takes of the mind to expect that I shall convince them all, or indeed so much as the greater part. But I confidently expect that such a proportion of all the people in the country will become sensible of the impolicy of the late act, as will procure us a repeal of it speedily in the ensuing Session of Parliament.

THE END.

C. and R. Baldwin, Printers,
New Bridge-street, London.